a journal

Prisoners' Wives, Girlfriends, & Partners (PWGP)
P. O. Box 14241
Norfolk, VA 23518

Separated by Prison, United by Conviction–A Journal.

Published and distributed in the United States by: Prisoners' Wives, Girlfriends, & Partners (PWGP), Inc., pwgp.org

ISBN: 9780615795980

To the millions of people who are the embodiment of commitment, supporting their partners and standing up for their relationships, knowing in the end nothing matters more than love.

To: ______________________________

From: ______________________________

Every person in every relationship simply wants to know– THEY MATTER!

I give you this journal because ______________________________

____

____

____

What I want to accomplish at the end of this journal is ______________________________

____

____

____

Start Date: ______________________________

Love ______________________________

contents

Introduction

Relationships in which one partner is incarcerated fail at a high rate. One doesn't need a statistic to know this. Spend a year in any prison visitation room and you'll see couples fall by the wayside year after year.

It's time to reverse this trend.

Relationships need to be cultivated and nurtured. If not, the end result is two people living in two different worlds. A relationship with a prison sentence in the middle is hard time. Even in the best of relationships, things stagnate and become routine: same call schedule, same visit time, same conversation. The incarcerated partner becomes relegated to the person on the phone, with no real input in his/her partner's life or outside world. Many couples are stuck in a rut, focused only on the day of release, without real plans for a life after incarceration. When that day comes, two strangers try to unify. Couples must prepare for a life together, not live a life apart.

If you are anything like the millions of partners in similar situations, you look for activities that not only keep you connected but also help pass the time. ***Separated by Prison, United by Conviction- a journal*** is designed with this purpose in mind.

In this journal, you'll find relationship questions similar to those found in other relationship journals. However, you'll also find questions relatable to your special circumstances and needs.

How to use the journal?

Separated by Prison, United by Conviction- a journal is intended to provoke couples to discuss their relationship. Use the questions as conversation starters or letter prompts. It's called a journal because in order to maximize your benefit from it, you need to write down what you feel.

The journal consists of five sections, the first three of which include questions for both of you, questions answered from the outside partner's point of view, and questions answered from the inside partner's point of view.

The "What Would You Do" section offers scenarios that might not be pertinent to your situation but present circumstances that allow partners to think outside themselves and share their thoughts and opinions, in order to learn something about each other that you didn't know. Ask "What would you do?" after each question. This is one time where it's appropriate to assume facts not in evidence.

The last section of the journal includes a few partner exercises to strengthen your bond and renew your commitment. Each page contains a "Heart Speak" quote. As you complete each page, discuss each quote and tell your partner how and why it speaks to your heart.

After you have completed the journal with your partner, take the "Healthy Relationship Pledge" and commit to a *quality* relationship despite your arrangement.

By the end of this journal, we hope you have shared laughs and gained insights, but more importantly we hope you have fallen more in love.

Questions for Couples

What is your definition of a healthy relationship?

What is your definition of a good partner?

What does commitment mean to you?

"Your laugh is the soundtrack of my heart."

Is there such a thing as "too much in love"?

What do you love most about your partner?

Should people in relationships have some level of privacy?

Who is the head of your family?

Relationships with people behind bars are "meaningful, but not fulfilling." Do you agree?

How do you handle arguments?

When you argue with your partner, do you argue to win or to be heard?

Do you feel that some arguing is healthy for your relationship? Do you feel that couples that argue are bound to fail?

Do you and your partner have different faiths? If so, how do you handle it?

Is your partner romantic? How?

Is it romantic for a guy to give flowers to a woman who hates flowers? Is romance a universal language or does it have to be taught?

Is love a decision or a feeling?

Is love and/or a relationship work?

Are warm and fuzzies required to be "in love"?

How can you be sure that you really love someone?

Describe your partner in one word.

When I think of my partner, I feel____________.

What are you sacrificing so your partner will feel loved?

Does it (the relationship) ever feel like an obligation?

What does your partner do that drives you insane?

Name something you do only because you know your partner likes it (as a way to honor him/her).

Have you taken on any of your partner's characteristics? Have you picked up on each other's phrases or mannerisms? How have you rubbed off on each other?

What has your partner done lately to make you feel loved?

Fill in the blanks. I am___________________. My partner is___________________.
Together, we are___________________.

What do you mean when you say, "It's worth it"?

What does loyalty mean to you?

Quote: Husbands have to be made. Do you agree?

Quote: Wives have to be made. Agree?

Besides sex, what is the one thing you really miss that you haven't been allowed?

I'm ok,
if you are ok.

How do you keep love alive in your relationship?

Do you believe people in relationships can be everything to each other?

Do you believe people in relationships should be everything to each other?

I wish tomorrow would hurry up, so I can remember how much I loved you today.

Ever feel like life is passing you by and you're stuck?

How would your life be different without this relationship?

How important is your relationship to you? Why is it important?

When loving someone through distance and time, what skills must one have?

Are the holidays worse than any other day or does it all feel the same?

Have you and your partner created a unique way to say "I Love You" without saying the words?

What does your partner say to you that makes your heart flutter?

What do you know about love today that you didn't know in your teens?

The most amazing thing about our love is__________________.

We hear all the time that communication is an essential part of a relationship. What is communication? How is it different from talking?

Do you feel comfortable expressing your feelings to your partner? Are you completely open, or do you hold back?

Are there certain topics you won't discuss over the phone or in a letter, topics you agree to postpone until you are able to see each other? Why?

You knew your partner was the one when ________________.

What are your insecurities and how have you learned to handle them?

What "little things" does your partner do for you that always seem to bring a smile to your face?

How do you put your "foot down"? How does your partner respond?

What kind of positive feedback have you received about your relationship? From whom did it come from?

What is something you do not want anyone to ever say about your relationship?

Have you ever let the stress of what others say affect your relationship? To what extent? What made you stop and realize how others feel is irrelevant or have you?

Is your partner a reflection of who you are as a person? Why or why not?

What will you NOT tolerate no matter what?

If you could only keep one memory of your life together, what would it be?

Does your partner bring up things he/she has "forgiven" you for? Do you think they have truly forgiven you or did they just say so in order to move on?

What have you found yourself forgiving your partner for that you never thought you would be able to?

What is something you feel you CANNOT ever forgive?

Are there things for which you need to forgive YOURSELF? What steps are you taking to achieve this?

What have you done to make this prison sentence bearable for each other?

Is there a difference between contentment and happiness? If so, what is the difference?

Is there a difference between loyalty and faithfulness? If so, what is the difference?

Is there a difference between sex and intimacy? If so, what is the difference? Do you prefer one over the other and why?

Even in the bleakest of worlds, there is hope.

Is there a difference between living and existing? If so, what is the difference? Can you exist and not live? Explain.

Is there a difference between love and like? If so, what is the difference? Can you love someone without liking them? Explain.

What is the difference between love and lust? Do you have to experience one to fully understand the other?

Hang tight!
It's going to be an exhilarating, terrifying, exciting, bumpy ride.

What is the difference between waiting on your partner and standing by your partner's side during this time? Are you waiting or standing?

What is your love language?

Kissing is like punctuation. It can be the end of a statement, a promise of things to come, or a full declaration. Think about your first kiss with your partner. Was it a period, comma, exclamation point, other?

Half Full vs. Half Empty. Everyone's situation is different. Do you consider your glass to be half full or half empty? Explain.

Truth vs. A lie. Do you prefer the truth at all costs or would you be okay with a lie to protect your feelings? Why?

Love vs. Obligation. Do you think these two are confused at times? Do you feel people stay in relationships because they feel obligated rather than because they are in love? Can you separate the two reasons?

Boyfriend/Girlfriend vs. Husband/Wife. Besides the legal document, what would you say separates the two? Do things change once you have transformed in to being the husband/wife? Explain. Why or why not?

Free World vs. Prison Relationships. Besides not having your partner free, do you feel there is a difference between the two types of relationships? If so, what is the difference? Is one easier than the other? Explain.

Infidelity. Emotional vs. Physical. Do you consider an emotional connection, without the physical one, to someone other than your partner as cheating? Which do you feel is worse? Why do you feel this way? Do you think you can forgive either?

Far Sighted vs. Near Sighted. Do you tend to focus more on what lies before you than on what is to come? Why do you think you look at things this way?

Protective vs. Controlling. “He doesn't want me going out. He is afraid something might happen to me.” “He chooses my friends.” “She doesn't think I should get another tattoo” “If he calls and I don't answer, he turns into a monster!” Are these controlling or protective statements? When does one turn in to the other?

Your Love vs. Their Love. "I love you more!" "No baby, I'm pretty sure I love you more!" Have you ever had cute little arguments over who loves and misses the other most? Who usually wins?

People who've been happily together for a long time also find there is room for growth in their relationships. When a relationship stops growing, it becomes stagnant and starts decaying. How do you and your partner continue to grow? How do you keep the focus on the two of you despite the circumstances?

What specific incident/event did you experience with your partner that helped you grow as a couple? How did this change the relationship?

List the ways you have grown since the beginning of this incarceration?

Define the word "commitment." What does it mean to you?

What change in your partner's attitude, behavior, or character would you like to see? Why do you believe a change is necessary?

How did you and your partner approach problems/issues in the beginning of your relationship? How do you approach them now? Is there a difference?

"*There* are two options regarding commitment. You're either in or out. There's no such thing as a life in-between." Agree or disagree? Why?

"*There's* a difference between interest and commitment. When you're interested in doing something, you do it only when circumstances permit. When you're committed to something, you accept no excuses, only results." Agree or disagree? Why?

For those who are married, how did you know you were ready to make the commitment?

For those who are not married, do you think you are ready to make the commitment of marriage? Why or why not?

Aside from being away from your partner, what would you say is the hardest challenge in a prison sentence?

Do you miss your partner more or less after a visit? Explain.

Which one of you is more patient?

Name a specific time or event when you had to show tremendous patience (besides the obvious).

True love is when you put someone on a pedestal but are there to catch them when they fall.

What is your biggest fear regarding your relationship, if any?

What are some "firsts" as a couple you've missed because of the incarceration?

Who is the "joketeller" in the relationship? What are some memorable funnies?

What is something you can say to your partner that only he/she would understand?

Describe a memorable time with your partner, an occasion a moment where you had tons of fun and just enjoyed each other, a moment where you laughed so hard you cried, an instance that makes you still smile when you think about it.

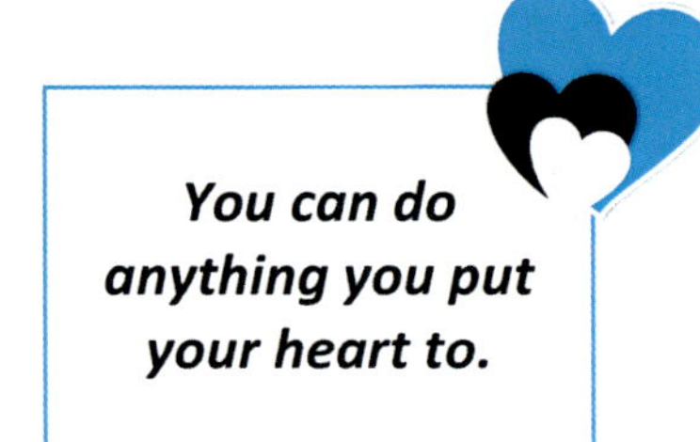

You can do anything you put your heart to.

If you are/ will marry while incarcerated, do you plan on having your dream wedding after release? Describe the wedding.

Were you and your partner friends before you started dating? How did you cross over into a full blown-relationship? Was it awkward at first? Was it easy because of the length of time you had been friends? Explain.

How much energy do you put in your relationship? Do you believe you could do a little more? Could your partner do a little more? If so, what more could you do and what more would like your partner to do?

Were you ever at a point where you had little faith in your partner? Why did you feel this way?

If your partner came with a "WARNING" label, what would it say?

What things work for you and your partner that wouldn't work for other couples?

My relationship with my partner is unique because ____________.

Write ONE rule or general statement to include in a handbook for men/women.

Have you ever held any resentment towards your partner? Why? How did it affect your relationship? If not, do you think holding resentment in a relationship could have enough power to affect it in a negative way?

Has your partner ever expressed any feelings of regret to you? If so, what is it that he/she regrets?

What is the craziest thing that you have done for "love?"

Name three things you need to work on.

Name three things that would make your relationship stronger.

Do you believe in divorce? Why or why not?

List all issues you believe married couples should make an honest attempt to work through and overcome. List all issues you feel can't be worked through.

If divorce was not an option, if all marriages were final, would you have married your partner? If you are not married yet, but you knew the marriage would be final and there is absolutely no way out regardless of circumstances. Would you still want to marry your partner? Why? Explain.

Can a relationship survive without trust? Explain.

How important is loyalty?

When you receive mail, do you open it right away? Do you wait until you are somewhere alone and read it? Do you find yourself reading it over and over again?

You have probably seen many relationships come and go. You have probably heard all types of horror stories. You have probably seen a lot of couples give up. Do you ever let this affect you? Do you ever wonder if this could happen to you? If so, how have you learned to deal with it?

Can a marriage/relationship truly survive without intimacy? Explain.

If your partner were home, would intimacy be important? Is sex more important than intimacy for the survival of a free-world marriage/relationship? Explain.

What annoys you about visitation?

What is your favorite part about preparing for a visit?

How do you usually feel when preparing for a visit? Are you excited or anxious? Do you still get butterflies? Describe your emotions.

Describe your very first visit, your emotions, thoughts, feelings.

During your visits are you the center of attention? Are you two in your own little worlds? What is a typical visit like for you and your partner?

Describe a memorable visit (I know it's all memorable). Which visit really stands out? Why?

What is your definition of a "perfect" visit?

What are your bad visits like? Do you sit quietly and talk things out? Are you loud? Do either of you leave the visit?

There is no storm strong enough to knock you off your game.

How do you feel after you visit your partner? Do you have the after-visit blues or a visit high? Describe.

What is the craziest thing you have witnessed in the visitation room? What was your reaction?

Do you have a monthly budget?

Do you classify the income as "my money" or "our money"?

I love my partner for the same reason I breathe. If I didn't, I would die.

"You can't truly take care of someone until you take care of yourself." Agree?

Besides your relationship, what is working well in your life that you wouldn't change?

What do you know now that you wish you had known at the beginning of this journey?

Here is your megaphone: What do you want to say to the world?

What have you learned about yourself during this time?

What are your expectations for homecoming? Describe your plans?

Do you believe you are"victims" of this life? Of the system? Why?

For those whose partners have been sentenced to twenty years or more, what keeps you fighting? How do you maintain the faith that one day, you two will have your happily ever after? How do you keep the "fight?"

What do you think will be the hardest challenge for you and your partner upon release?

They say, "It's not a real relationship. You don't have the irritations of day-to-day life, with bills, housework, and kids." I say, "You are letting your ignorance show." What do you say?

If you were offered a year of family visits*, but it would extend the release date by six months, would you take it?

Questions for Outside Partner:

Are you making this life harder than it has to be?

Do you put up with things from your partner that you wouldn't normally tolerate because he or she is in prison?

*Family visits- Extended private visits offered in six states.

What has been the greatest obstacle of your partner's incarceration?

Do you worry that prison is making your partner worse?

If another unrelated person the same sex as you visits your partner (without you), do you consider this cheating?

Is there is a difference between loving someone incarcerated vs. loving someone free? If so, what is the difference? If not, why do you think there is no difference?

As a child you probably didn't imagine you'd be married to or date someone incarcerated. Despite this disconnect between what you imagined and what really happened, has your relationship with your partner turned out to be everything you have ever dreamed? How?

What makes your partner special? Why is he/she worth all you deal with in the world?

What do you think has been your partner's biggest adjustment in prison (besides the obvious of being away from home and the world)?

In a typical marriage/relationship, many of life's day to day decisions are made together. Having an incarcerated partner can hinder this process. Does your partner have a say in the daily decisions of the home? How do you keep your partner connected and feeling important?

Some partners on the outside lose their individuality and become all about their incarcerated partner. They become consumed with prison life as a whole. What do you do to assure you do not lose yourself in your partner or in the prison life? How do you maintain your sanity?

How many bids* are you willing to do?

Do you tell your partner everything that happens while he/she is gone or do you keep the hurtful/upsetting things to yourself?

In the beginning did you find yourself telling "white lies" to cover up the truth? Were you ashamed of your partner's location at anytime during your journey? Explain. Why or why not?

There is nothing worse than a quiet house when you are waiting on someone.

What is the biggest change you have seen in your partner since incarceration? Was this change for the good or the bad?

**Bid- prison sentence*

What is the biggest change you have noticed in yourself since your partner's incarceration? Was this change for the good or for the bad?

Missing you reminds me I have a reason to rejoice, for I am loved.

Do you have faith your partner will return a changed person for the better?

Do you trust your partner not to return to prison once he/she is released? Why?

Does your partner ever speak/hold conversations with other inmates during visitation? If so, does this bother you?

I am not a stereotype because ___________.

Do you feel like you have to know everything about your partner, such as who visits, who is on his or her call list? Do you want copies of all his or her correspondence? It's the prison equivalent of going through his wallet, cell phone, etc. Some call it honesty. Some call it a lack of trust. What do you think?

Are you willing to give your partner an adjustment period after release, i.e., a time to sow his/her wild oats?

Describe this experience of having an incarcerated partner in ONE word.

Questions for Incarcerated Partner:

How has your incarceration affected your relationship?

Do you feel isolated and alone? How does your partner help ease these feelings?

Are there certain topics you would rather not discuss in a call or a letter?

Some people say there is no such thing as an "ex"- con. Agree? Why or why not?

Have you been changed by this incarceration? How and has the change been for the better or for the worse?

If you had a chance to make this right (situation, incarceration), what would you do?

Will you try to make up for lost time when released or will you pick up where you are?

Your partner is waiting for you, while you are waiting for the world. Upon your release, how will you ensure your partner does not feel his or her efforts were in vain?

In addition to guilt by association, your partner may have been shunned or ostracized for loving you. How do you feel about this and if this is the case, what have you done or do you plan to do to help your partner through this?

What have you learned about yourself doing this time?

How many bids are you willing to do?

If your partner were incarcerated, would you wait and if so, would you wait with the same expectations you have placed on her/him now?

Do you experience PMS (Prison Mood Swings)? If so, what are they like for you?

What is your greatest fear regarding your relationship and the incarceration?

What do you need to say to your partner? What would you like your partner to say to you?

"You have no room to complain. You put yourself there!" "You should have thought about this before you decided to go to prison!" Has your partner ever spoken to you like this? How does it make you feel? What do you think your partner is really saying? How do you respond to statements such as these?

"I think I have it harder than you do! You never have to worry about where your next meal is coming from. You have no bills. I am the one doing everything!" Has your partner said these things to you? How does it make you feel? What do you think your partner is really saying? How do you respond to statements such as these?

What are your expectations (for life, relationship) during this incarceration and upon release?

Are you afraid of the unknown? The closer you get to a release date, do you feel anxiety? Will you try to sabotage the relationship because you are afraid everything in your life is going to change again?

Love passionately!

What is the one thing you are especially looking forward to doing when you get home (besides sex)?

Have you tried to push your partner away? If so, why.

Have you ever felt your partner deserved more than this? Why? Have you discussed this with your partner, and if so, how has your partner responded?

What would your partner say if asked why you are worth the wait?

Tell your partner why you are worth the wait.

> ***Fairytales do co[me] true. All you need i[s] two people with a desire to live happily ever after. The location of each person is irrelevant.***

What Would You Do?

His partner does not eat pork. The prison serves a lot of pork items. She goes on a hunger strike and refuses all food. He can't afford to send her money to eat commissary items only. She is upset, says he doesn't care, and declares that if he loved her, he would find a way.

Her partner has been in the hole four times in the past five years. His disciplinary action will factor in to his parole. She is upset. Each time he goes to the hole, he reduces his chances of coming home sooner than later. Should there be any consequences (from her)?

Her partner is wrongfully convicted. In order for him to make parole, he must show remorse. He says, he will never admit to a crime he didn't commit. He will not apologize. She is frustrated. She wants him to do whatever he can to come home, but must respect his wishes.

Her partner is offered a plea deal for something he did not do. The offer is twelve years. If he goes to trial and loses, he faces up to thirty-five years. He has prior convictions. The evidence is circumstantial, but can go either way. Does she advise him to take the deal or roll the dice, or does she stay out of it and allow him to make the decision?

She is invited to a family gathering. Out of respect for her partner, she declines, refusing to put herself in a situation where her relationship will not be respected. Her family member gets upset, insisting there is nothing wrong with socializing with other men. Her response, "The only man I need to socialize with is my fiancé."

His partner is up for parole two years before her max date. He feels she needs more time to fully rehabilitate. Would you encourage her to stay the two years?

Partner comes home after ten years and says, "Baby, I still love you and really want to be with you, but you have let yourself go." He gives you a time frame to get yourself together or he's leaving.

Husband is up for parole soon. Due to his gang affiliations, he has been in trouble five times in the past two months. She is furious. She sees this as his putting prison stuff before their family.

Wife smuggles in contraband. She is caught. She is banned for visiting any prison. She is charged. A conviction carries up to three years. Husband says, he has nothing to do with it. If she is convicted, he wants a divorce.

Husband has been out of prison a year. He hasn't found a job. He's depressed, spending less time looking for work. Wife is frustrated; upset she is still carrying the family after his eight years of incarceration. To her, he is no longer trying, after she busted her butt for years to stay afloat. She feels he is playing the victim.
She is considering separation.

Partner has been home a few months. He's fine during the day but at night, while sleeping, he is violent. Whenever she touches him, he lashes out. She's had a black eye and swollen lip because of it.

Some guys, he met while locked up, start calling and wanting to hang out. You don't want to choose his friends for him, but it is a violation of parole. How do you handle the situation?

After a twelve year sentence, he was released to his wife and children. Six months in, he has not been able to find employment and has voiced to his wife that he is sick of watching her struggle to take care of the family. Shortly after he is pampering her and the kids. She has an idea as to how, but is scared to confirm. What does she do if he has returned to his old ways? How does she handle it?

Her partner was paroled a year ago. They had a huge argument and that same night, he re-offended.
He is looking at minimum five years in prison. She feels guilty. "Had I not argued with him that night, we wouldn't be facing this, right?" She doesn't think she can do five more years, but feels obligated.

After doing a thirteen year bid, her boyfriend comes home a week earlier than expected and does not inform her. He spends this week away getting "everything out of his system. " He is ready to come home. She is aware of everything her partner has been up to. She is hurt. Her partner is apologetic and promises to make up for it. Forgive and forget?

Her fiancé wants "feel good" photos but she is uncomfortable with her body. She has issues with her mid-section and dreaded cellulite. He says that there is nothing wrong with her body and loves her regardless. He is unhappy she won't send photos. She believes she is disappointing him by not doing what he likes, but her body image issues are real for her. How would you handle this?

In a marriage, "for worse" often comes after "for better."

Woman meets man through pen pal site. They plan to get married in a few months. She is the happiest she has ever been, except for one thing. He will not share the details of his conviction. He told her, "It's private." She doesn't want to lose him.

If this were about longing, I would be fine. If this were about missing, I would get by. This is about going through life knowing something is not right.

She marries her pen pal and has been approved for family visits. She wants to take her kids on this visit, both of whom do not want to go. She insists, saying it's time for them to meet their new dad.

Man has been in prison eight years. His girlfriend was pregnant at the time of his arrest. She stops bringing their son to visits, saying that it's an unhealthy environment for him. She doesn't want the child to see prison as an option. He hasn't seen his son in four years.

Couple has been dating five years. Two weeks before his release, he requests "space". She says, "Five years is plenty of space." He says, "I need time to adjust." He wants to move in with his brother to get used to being free, but says he will come home as soon as he feels ready.

Her partner has kids with another woman. Per her request, his children's mother is not added to his phone/visit list. He wants to parent his kids. The mother of his kids will not allow contact without being involved. Your partner requests the two women move in together and visit as a group.

Her partner comes home after twelve years. New home. New furniture. New neighborhood. He finds it difficult to be in "her" world. She has a hard time relinquishing control. She is trying to help, but he sees it as giving orders. They argue all the time. How do they fix this?

Husband has been home for two years. They have decided to have their first child. They each have a full physical. Husband's blood tests positive for HIV. Wife's tests negative. Devastated, she is not sure she still wants a child. He has not revealed how he contracted it. They were together before his incarceration.

Woman is serving an LWOP* sentence plus fifty years. She's been writing a pen pal for over a year. She wants to marry. He is hesitant. He wants to be a dad. He tells her, "All I've ever wanted is to be a father." She is hurt and wonders if he really loves her. He thinks she is being selfish, asking him to give up his dreams for hers.

Every time he calls, girlfriend feels she is being interrogated. He wants to know where she has been, with whom, why, etc. He requests a list of her daily activities. He says if he were home, he would know where she always was and thus he is entitled to know now. She says he is too controlling and is being unreasonable.

During a visit, wife screams when she sees a cockroach. Guard says, "Don't act like you haven't seen a roach before." Husband gets angry at the guard's remark and is sent to the hole for defending his wife. Wife vows not to come back to the "filthy prison again." Husband is irritated.

**LWOP- Life Without Parole*

Husband and wife split two years in to his sentence. Both are dating others. Husband is being released in five months after serving eight years. He wants to stay with wife until he gets on his feet. He has nowhere else to go. His wife feels he's not her responsibility. They are not officially divorced.

Husband is up for parole next month. His max date is in a year. Wife wants husband to max out so he will be released free and clear. He disagrees but will do it to please her. She wonders if she is being selfish.

She says, "After four years in prison, he came back big and bitter. I loved the man who went to prison but not the man who came home." She says he didn't try to better himself. All he did was lift weights all day. She feels they are no longer on the same level. They are not married. Is she obligated to work it out? Does she owe it to him?

Husband has been in prison fifteen years. While inside he became a "prison wife." He is being released in three months. He is leaving his wife for his "prison husband," who was released two years prior. The real wife is furious and hurt, but doesn't believe in divorce.

Husband and wife were both Christian. Husband converted to Islam while in prison. Wife is upset. She says they are no longer "equally yoked" and feels the different faiths will ruin the marriage.

Boyfriend receives LWOP sentence. His girlfriend wants to marry him. Parents of the girl will not give their consent for their daughter to get married. The girlfriend is sixteen, and the boyfriend is eighteen.

Wife is growing increasingly tired. She feels unappreciated. She is "this close" to letting it all go. She is no longer happy. The only thing stopping her is that she has invested so much time and energy over past ten years. She feels stuck and doesn't know what to do.

He has been free for two weeks. He is happy and adjusting well. However, she is realizing it is not all she had dreamed. She says he is too clingy. She says maybe she fell in love with the "bad boy." She is thinking of ending the relationship but doesn't want to hurt him.

Her partner has been incarcerated for over a year. At first she didn't visit out of anger, now she isn't visiting because she is scared to face the reality of the whole thing. She prefers to remember him as he was before.

She writes an inmate and a relationship blossoms. They are "head over heels" in love and plan to marry. She finds out that the man she has been writing to isn't the man she has pictures of, but is his cell mate.

e worst thing that happened to you can be the best thing, if you let it.

Husband wants wife to stay seated when on a visit. He says he doesn't want her prancing around with other men looking at her. She says he is being unreasonable and overprotective.

During a visit you notice a woman and child. The woman uses all her money on snacks for her partner. Her child is now crying for a snack. She asks to borrow money from you. Do you volunteer even if she doesn't ask?

They share info about household finances. He helps with budget. They figure out where the money is going and when. He requests bank statements and receipts for everything she spends (even for a trip to Wal-Mart). He says he wants to know where all money is going. She says he wants to clear the way for more commissary money.

Being in a relationship with someone incarcerated is the subtle art between living and dying.

Inmate is in prison for crime involving kids. His visit sheet is tagged, "Not allowed around children." During visitation with his wife, another couple is not watching their daughter. The child is playing and running around close to the inmate. His wife returns the little girl to her family, but the little girl comes back. The inmate's visit is terminated.

Wife says, "Not a day goes by that I don't apologize for leaving my family." She feels horrible for the pain she has caused by putting them in this position. "I will always feel I owe him the world. How do I stop being so hard on myself and know his feelings and love will never die or change? He says he will wait forever."

Wife receives a letter from a woman. She confronts her husband. He informs her he writes numerous women, but only for financial support. He believes that in doing so, he is "taking the burden off his wife" He is apologetic. Wife is furious.

Husband has been locked up two months. Wife is having a hard time adjusting. Everyone she meets keeps saying "Think about what he is going through." She understands his hardships but is tired of people making it all about his pain as if her pain doesn't matter.

Husband and wife are in the eighth year of a fifteen year bid. In the beginning, wife wrote every day, sent lots of cards, visited every week, and made sure his commissary was full. She also went out of her way to make sure he felt like the man of the house. Now, she has no time to visit, writes on a whim, and barely mentions things going on in her life. The husband feels unwanted and alone even though his wife insists she still loves him and can't wait for him to come home.

Husband comes home. Everything is great. Months later, he tells his wife that while in prison, he slept with men--- voluntarily in order to get by.

Partner Exercises

Complete the following exercises individually then discuss as a couple.

Who am I?

Being in a relationship with a prison sentence is difficult. Knowing who you are and being grounded in that knowledge is important when dealing with the rigors of this lifestyle.

In this exercise, list your core values (faith, honesty, loyalty)—the heart of who you. Draw a line from the value that helps you combat and overcome negative influences.

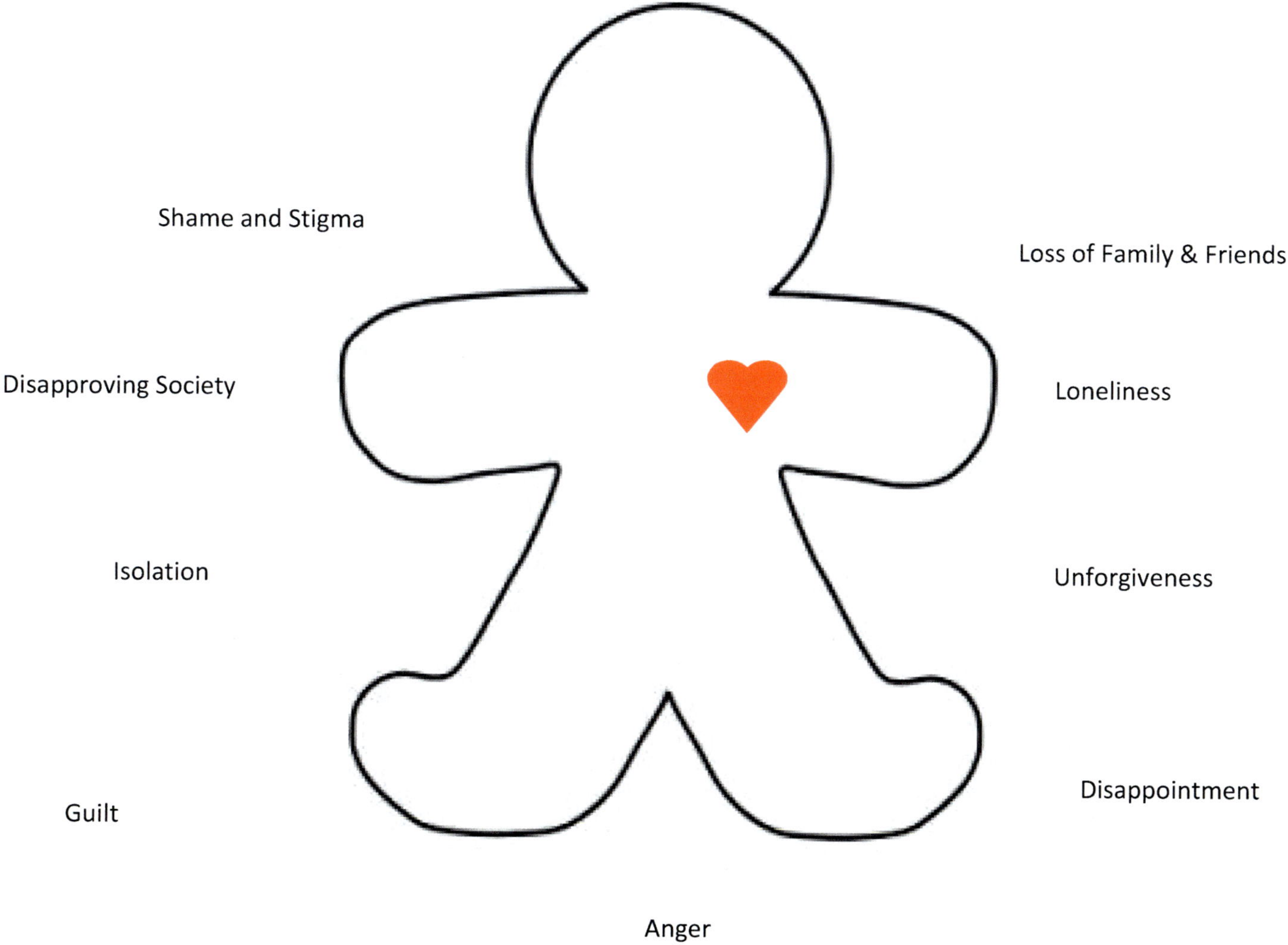

Experiences

List the experiences that shaped your life as a girl, an adolescent, and a woman. Describe how these experiences affect you and your partner.

Experiences

List the experiences that shaped your life as a boy, an adolescent, and a man. Describe how these experiences affect you and your partner.

Strengths and Weaknesses

We all have strengths and weaknesses shaped by our experiences.

In this exercise, list your strengths and weaknesses. Discuss how this will help or hinder your relationship.

Strengths

____

____

____

____

How will your strengths help or hinder this experience?

____

____

Weaknesses

____

____

____

____

How will your weaknesses help or hinder this experience?

____

____

For the next thirty days, write down one thing you love, appreciate, enjoy, think or feel about your partner. Mail it with a title: Thirty Reasons Why I Love You, Thirty Reasons Why I Will Never Leave, Thirty Reasons Why You Are Worth It.

Write your relationship mission statement.

Write a "Romantic Resume." Apply for the job of being with your partner. Outline your qualifications and your skills. Include a cover letter. Send this to your partner. Wait to be called for an interview where your partner will ask the following questions:

- *Why* are you interested in the posted position?
- *What* type of experience do you have?
- *What* did you like or dislike about your previous job (partner)?
- *What* are your salary expectations? (What do you expect to receive from the relationship?)
- *Why* should we hire you? What sets you above all of the other applicants?

Write your relationship annual Check Up: Things I am, Things I'm not. Things I will. Things I need.

(See examples in appendix.)

The End of the journal

Hopefully, a new beginning for you

Keep fighting the good fight!

Appendix A

Relationship Mission Statement

Many businesses and organizations have a mission statement. Management often refers to it to ensure their actions adhere to what they said they would do. The company culture is governed by this statement and thus becomes the law of the land.

Relationships can benefit from such a statement. Sure, you vow to love, honor, [obey], be together forever and ever, but how do you get to the forever part?

What is the goal of the union?

What do you want to achieve?

What rules do you want to abide by?

What example do you want to set?

Here is an example of a mission statement:

The Thompson Family union is our strength, power, and fortitude to deal with life's up and downs. Our marriage is designed by us and is not governed by influences of society or religious references, unless we choose. Our union is one hundred percent of each of us. It is a safe haven, a place where masks are not needed, but where different faces are encouraged. Our support of each other empowers us to be ourselves stripped to the bone. Our mission is to love each other in a place where space and time does not exist. We continue to live by the concept of "WillReese."*No one half is greater than the whole.* We will respect and encourage each other's growth and development as individuals, because our strength as a couple relies on our separate, but equal, abilities. We are a couple who inspires others with our life and love and who model what it is to be in a great relationship.

Appendix B

Relationship Resume

Ever thought of applying for the job of being with your partner? Relationships can be work. You can make this as basic or as detailed as you want. Go apply for those positions. I have a feeling you will be hired on the spot.

Cover Letter

Please find enclosed my resume for the position of Love of Your Life.

I believe my skills and experience are a good match to the criteria for this position. I have extensive experience in dating and relating to the opposite sex. I'm a team player and love the benefits of being in a relationship.

I believe I can make a positive contribution to this position. I look forward to the opportunity to work with and under you.

Please contact me should you require any additional information.

Resume

Objective:

To obtain the position of Love of Your Life.

Summary:

Promoted to the position of fiancé, after a couple months of dating, being friends and laying a foundation. A year later, I obtained the highest honor of being your wife.

Education:

- School of Hard Knocks, Class of Yesterday and Today
- Masters in the ART of being me
- Masters in Prisoner's Wife-ology
- Degrees in Ambition, Stress, Self-Improvement
- Currently enrolled in Life Experience Training

Experience:

With over twenty-three years dating experience and six years of marriage, I've held positions as a friend, girlfriend, and wife. Responsibilities include: couple appearances, supporting partner, ego-stroking, keeping a home, relations, mothering, friendship, mind-reading, arguing, hearing and listening and other duties as assigned.

Achievements:

- Nine years of being a prisoner's wife.
- Gained self-confidence, assurance, and reliance.
- Know all of your favorites.
- Perfected being the "ying" to your "yang".

Skills:

- Aerobics instructor (need I list more)

References furnished upon request.

Appendix C

Relationship Annual Checkup

As your union matures, your wants and needs change. Perform an annual checkup on your relationship. Strip down to the core of yourself and share with your partner where you are in the moment.

Relationship Annual Checkup Example:

Things I am:
I am a handful, dramatic, overbearing, & stubborn. I am still mourning the death of a dream.
I am ready for a traditional life.
I am *that* chick, *any* chick.

Things I am not:
I am not without flaws. In fact, as the years pass, some seem to get worse I am not as happy as I seem.
I am not easy.
I am not the same chick you married six years ago.

Things I will:
I will continue to make the most of a less than ideal situation. I will hold it down, until you can take over.
I will support and encourage you.
I will play my position.
I will love you like none other.

Things I won't:
I will not make promises I can't keep. I will not hide how I feel.
I will not tolerate anything that jeopardizes your freedom.

Things I can't:
I cannot change the way the world views you.
I cannot be responsible for your happiness but I can continue to do those things that create that feeling for you.
I cannot live on a pedestal. If you continue to put me there, you must promise to catch me when I fall. I cannot love you past your pain, but I can love you to a place where your pain is less relevant.
I cannot set you free.

Things I need:
I need you to be patient. I don't have all the answers. I need to feel special.

Will you accept all these things I am, am not, will, will not, cannot, and need?

Healthy Relationship Pledge

I promise to love honor and respect my partner and to realize that our relationship is not defined by pressures of society nor the location of either partner. I promise to overcome any barriers that may hinder the growth and stability of a healthy, strong family unit, up to and including seeking help outside myself. I realize that I can only be responsible for my actions, and that to change a relationship, I must first change myself. I realize that a healthy relationship includes two healthy people. I will love honor and respect myself first so the promise I made in the first sentence not only will be true but also the law of this partnership, because our goal is to keep this family together no matter what.

____
Committed Partner

____
Reesy Floyd-Thompson, Founder & President of PWGP
Self-Esteem & Relationship Coach

____
Date

About the Founder

Reesy Floyd-Thompson stood behind her husband, Nivens Thompson, in a Pennsylvania courtroom and watched as the love of her life was sentenced to 12 ½ to 25 years. Her life changed forever. There was never a question as to if she would keep her commitment to him — she'd made that decision months before when she said "until death do us part." For better or worse, she would never go back to simply being Mrs. Thompson. Now, she was also Mrs. GE-6309, the wife of a prisoner with a different kind of existence.

The first few years of the sentence, Reesy grieved the loss of her husband, the loss of her dreams. She went through the motions of answering the calls, writing the letters, and visiting. She told Nivens everything he needed to hear. She loved him. She would wait for him. She couldn't live without him. Though she didn't believe her own words, she played her part. As the years passed by, the harder it became. Reesy lost herself in the process of keeping Nivens relevant in the world. She straddled the line between Mrs. Thompson and Mrs. GE-6309. She talked about Nivens all the time to her closest friends and family, but sometimes the story of Nivens and his incarceration did not fit in to her life. A new job with a new set of friends and suddenly having a husband in prison was not acceptable. During this time, Reesy searched for support groups for her situation. For a while she participated in online groups, but she couldn't spend her life in front of a computer. Eventually, she found an in-person group for families of the incarceration. As she sat there, she listened as the facilitator mentioned every familial relationship except husband and wife. When was it going to be okay to mention the anger she felt over Nivens' absence or the resentment she harbored for his leaving her alone? Her friends were good sounding boards, but they didn't really understand the loneliness, isolation, or hopelessness she felt. They couldn't feel the frustration of the struggle to maintain an identity, while being swallowed up by all things prison related. During this time, Reesy and Nivens marriage was strained. Going through the motions took its toll on the relationship. She needed a place to vent about a lifestyle in which she didn't know how to adjust.

In 2009, Reesy held a meeting in a local library for what was then called, "The Prisoner's Wife Club." Today, that club is now known as Prisoners' Wives, Girlfriends, & Partners (PWGP), a company that produces resources for those separated by prison. PWGP is one of the few organizations that exclusively addresses this population. As the founder of PWGP, Reesy is passionate about making sure that partners entering this lifestyle have immediate support. Though PWGP helps thousands of people, Reesy is helped most of all. Reesy is an advocate for partners standing up for their relationships during times of incarceration. She understands the hardship imprisonment places on a relationship. She has traveled across the country to meet other prisoners' partners for encouragement and support. She urges partners to be diligent in seeking and sharing the necessary resources to keep their families intact.

Through her work with PWGP, she has partnered with national and regional prison advocacy organizations. She is listed as a family member expert on the pilot program of Norfolk, Virginia's Prisoner Re-Entry Council. In this position, she works with the city to develop programs to assist prisoners upon return to society.

Her prison credentials include: former editor for the *InsideOut* newsletter for the Virginia CURE; contributing writer for *Graterfriends* for Pennsylvania Prison Society; creator and editor of popular blog *Mrs. GE-6309 Time* and host of podcast of the same name (now in archives).

Her work has been featured in local, regional, and online publications, including a featured article in the First Person Arts Museum: *Through the Bars: A Workshop on Objects and Memorials for Individuals Affected by Incarceration.* She has been interviewed for numerous television and radio shows. She is a certified life coach and marriage counselor. Norfolk, Virginia is her home.

Reesy & Nivens Thompson are nine years in to their sentence. Their marriage is stronger than ever.

Separated by Prison, United by Conviction
Review Form

Please tell us what you thought of this journal.

What did you like about the journal?

____

____

What didn't you like about the journal?

____

____

Did the journal help your relationship? How?

____

____

Would you like to see another volume?

____

____

More Thoughts

____

____

____

____

____

Mail review to:
PWGP
P. O. Box 14241
Norfolk, VA 23518
pwgp.org

Leave a review at pwgp.org in the *Stop by and Say Hello* section.

Made in the USA
Coppell, TX
16 April 2026